Mark Falls, PhD
5755 Mountain Hawk Dr. Suite 201 Santa Rosa, CA 95409
(707) 525-9300 markfallsphd@gmail.com

© 2017 by Mark Falls, PhD. All rights reserved

No part of this book may be reproduced in any form or by any electronic or mechanical means, including information storage and retrieval systems, without written permission from the author, except by a reviewer who may quote brief passages in a review.

First edition.

Foreward by Uriah Guilford, MFT

I consider Mark to be a trusted friend and a respected colleague. He has a tremendous amount of experience and expertise with substance abuse, teens & families. In fact, he is my go-to-guy when I am working with challenging clients and tough situations.

We have been collaborating together for a number of years and have found success in supporting families dealing with teen substance abuse.

Mark is a straight shooter and has a direct approach that works well with his clients. However, he is also compassionate, humorous and extremely committed to the families he works with.

I was pleased when he accepted my challenge to write this book. I felt strongly that his unique approach needed to be documented and shared with as many people as possible.

This book is direct and concise with practical advice. I know that you will benefit from learning these step-by-step strategies to prevent or interrupt your teen's drug use.

Acknowledgements

I would like to thank three people who have been instrumental in making this book possible. First and forever, my wife Dana, for her love, constant encouragement and for believing I had something to say. Second, my editor and sister-in-law, Allison Zuehlsdorff for her patience and kindness, her sharp eye and for making my writing sound better than it should. And lastly, Uriah Guilford, to whom I owe much gratitude for initially coming up with the idea: "You should write a book." He has been inspirational in so many ways.

Table of contents

Introduction

Chapter 1

What's the problem? Experimentation-Use-Abuse-Addiction

Chapter 2

How do we know who will develop a substance use disorder?

Chapter 3

Talking isn't working, but is "rehab" really the next step?

Chapter 4

The Treatment Continuum

Chapter 5

The Benefit of the Doubt Approach

Chapter 6

Drug Testing 101

You think your son or daughter is using drugs and/or alcohol. You have seen signs and found evidence that is impossible to explain any other way. You don't know what to do. Should I ask him/her? Should I call our family doctor? Should I call a therapist? Should I call the police? Should I move to a new city?

Questions and worries ramble furiously through your mind.

- *Maybe it's just a phase and we can wait it out.*

- *Maybe I really didn't see what I thought I saw, maybe it **was** oregano in the baggie. But why would my son have a bag of oregano in his room?*

- *Maybe I'm worrying needlessly. After all, what kid doesn't experiment with drugs and alcohol? I did.*

This book is designed to answer these questions and provide you with a tried and true action plan to address your teen's substance abuse behavior.

Important note: Throughout this book the word "drug (s)" refers to all mind and mood altering substances, including alcohol.

Introduction

During the 2000 days of adolescence important physical, emotional and cognitive growth takes place. It can be a deeply fulfilling and exhilarating time for you and your teen. It can also be accompanied by uncertainty, confusion and worry. Even under the best of circumstances, when drugs and alcohol are sprinkled into the mix of adolescence, worry can sometimes become flat-out terror.

Perhaps you've heard or even been found yourself muttering the adage, "Kids don't come with manuals". While this is true in the literal sense, this book is designed to guide you through the mine field of your child's substance "experimentation-use-abuse-addiction" cycle. Additionally, the *in-home intervention strategy*, Benefit of the Doubt, which you will read about in chapter 5, can often pre-empt the need for more intensive and expensive treatments.

Years ago I started a presentation series for parents called "Not My Kid". The theme was based on a study that showed that 80% of parents think teenage substance abuse is a serious and growing problem in society. On the other hand, the study indicated that only

16% of parents thought *their* child was at risk. The study begged the question "Then whose kids are those with the drug/alcohol problems?" What was most interesting to me was what a hard sell it ended up being (the presentations were free!) to school administrators and parent groups. Problem? What problem?

I have been working in the field of adolescent substance use disorders and treatment for the past 30 years. In that time, I have talked a grand total of *zero* kids out of liking their drugs. What I *have* been able to do is to help parents engineer an environment that makes using drugs and alcohol as uncomfortable and inconvenient as possible for their son or daughter. I have been able to help these parents prevent the suffering and heartache that accompanies substance use disorders, for both their child and themselves.

In those same 30 years I have had only five or six calls directly from kids interested in treatment. None of them followed through. By and large kids don't think they have a problem, especially in the early stages of drug use. For that reason, I prefer to think of adolescent substance abuse treatment as more focused on *training parents* and helping them to find their backbones and discover the motivation to do the hard work of getting in front of the moving freight train that is their child's drug use.

I don't fix kids, I rehab parents.

Chapter 1
What's the problem? Experimentation-Use-Abuse-Addiction

Several months ago I got a call from a mother who said " I got your name from a friend who used you to help her son. Our situation is much different though; her son was out of control. My son is 16 and I think he experiments a little and I want to be sure it doesn't go any further". I asked her some questions about what she knew about her son's drug and alcohol use. She said her son had been caught with pot at school in the 7th grade, was suspended for 3 days and promised to stop smoking. The mother went on to say she had found some empty beer cans in her son's closet, and an empty bottle of vodka in the garbage. She said her son's grades had gone down this year and that he tends to sleep often after school. Throughout the call she emphasized "I have talked to him many times about the dangers of taking drugs. I don't know why he continues to do it".

This is a fairly typical first phone call from a parent. In the example above it was reasonable (at first) for the mother to see her son's substance use as an example of what teenagers do; *explore and experiment.* However, from her story, it was clear that her son was past the experimentation phase.

Experimentation

By definition, experimentation is learning *what causes what effect.* Most people, even teenagers, are one or two trial learners, meaning, it only takes a time or two of doing something to know what it's about. Imagine never having played ping pong and your neighbor invites you to come over to play. The first hit or two tells you the game's basic objective; you are *experimenting* with the feel of the paddle in your hand and how it feels when you hit the ball. From there you are *using* the paddle and playing, albeit poorly, and honing your skills.

It is the same with teenage drug experimentation which represents a very small window in time. Once passed, the **use** phase starts.

Use

Drug **use** is knowing what the drug does (more or less) and then doing it to get the effect it produces. It is important to note that **experimentation-use** does not represent a sky-is-falling-problem necessarily. In fact, most teens and adults stay at this stage and never progress further. However, the dilemma is that we don't know who will stop and who will progress to **abuse**.

Abuse

Drug **abuse** is the stage when the effect of the substance is known (as seen in the **use** stage) ***and found to be highly pleasurable.*** From there the teenager becomes interested in getting *more* of that feeling and correspondingly the frequency and amount of the drugs used increases.

I received this email from my referral line:

"We have caught our daughter with marijuana a couple times. She assured us she had stopped and we just drug tested her but she tested positive. She is telling us now that there is nothing wrong with smoking it. We have addiction problems in our family."

This email is a good example of a teen who is creeping into the **abuse** stage.

- She has used drug(s): **experimentation**.
- She knows how it feels: **use.**
- She likes the feeling and wants to experience more of it: **abuse**

Addiction

Drug **addiction** is marked by the person's inability to stop the use of the substance. By now the brain has developed a *tolerance (needs more of the substance to get the same effect)* to the substance. Discontinuing the use of the substance, at this point, causes symptoms of *withdrawal* (physical discomfort) which the user can most easily alleviate by using more of the substance. This creates a self-perpetuating cycle which is the hallmark feature of addiction.

Note: MOST TEENS do not progress to addiction and stay or stop somewhere in the **experimentation-use**

stages. However, once a teen enters the **abuse-addiction** stages, interrupting the substance use momentum becomes more and more difficult.

Anecdotal clinical reports suggest that most teens have been using, on average, a year prior to the parents finding out about it. Add another 3 to 6 months before parents decide to call for help and by the time the parents are sitting in a therapist's office, enough time has elapsed for the teen's substance abuse behavior to become fairly well developed and entrenched.

The bad news, at this point, is the drug problem has had a chance to blossom. The good news is that the evidence that drug use is problematic is plentiful enough to now motivate the parents to move into action.

Chapter 2

How do we know who will develop a substance use disorder?

In the previous chapter it was noted that the majority of teenagers don't develop a substance use problem. In fact, statistics suggest that only about 1 in 10/12 people who use substances develops a **substance use disorder.**

The question is who makes up that 10 to 12%?

The other day I interviewed father and mother about their daughter's drug use. The father didn't think his daughter had a problem. "Come on, I smoked pot when I was in high school and I turned out ok. Besides, if we make a big deal of this it will only cause her to rebel and use more. It's a phase, that's what kids do".

Someday there will be lasers with the ability to probe into a person's brain to determine if he/she will develop a drug problem. Until then, the collection of "indicators" listed below is the best probe available, at this point, to help identify a person's risk.

Age of onset: The younger a child is when they start using drugs, the greater the risk.

Mental health problems: Anxiety, depression, ADHD, learning differences, etc.

Medical problems: Chronic or acute medical disorders of any kind.

Trauma: Poverty, abuse, neglect, bonding and attachment problems.

Family dysfunction: Persistent conflict including yelling, swearing, physical/emotional abuse, avoidance, and parents' substance use and/or mental health problems.

Family history: While there is no "alcohol gene", the chances of a teen developing a substance use problem is 60% if one parent has a substance use disorder and up to 80% if both parents have one.

Environment/opportunity: Because teens are wired to be curious and to explore what's novel in their world, having access and opportunity to use drugs increases risk.

The following checklist, used in conjunction with the indicators listed above, can also be helpful:

- Decline in school performance
- Conflict with parents or family members
- Behavioral problems; lying, stealing (home and/or school)
- Involvement with police and/or juvenile justice system
- Drugs/alcohol found (home, room, car etc..)
- Decreased interest in activities previously enjoyed
- New group of friends
- Unwillingness to discuss parent's concern about drug/alcohol use.

If two or more indicators are present the teen is at risk and intervention and/or treatment of some kind will be needed. However, there are situations where no indicators are present and yet the drug abuse is in full flight. These assessment tools, while far from perfect, are the best means of determining the probability of a teen developing a substance use disorder.

Early Intervention

Because it's not known, with any degree of certainty, which teen will develop a substance use disorder, it is imperative that parents jump in to interrupt the drug use pattern no matter the perceived amount of drug use or risk. If parents do not do everything within their power to redirect this path and their teen ends up being in the 10% of the population who develops a substance use disorder, parents will ultimately look back regretting their inaction.

Actions Parents Should Take Immediately

The primary goal of parenting a teen is to get them launched into the next phase of their lives successfully. When it is clear to the parents that their teen has a developing drug problem, parents need to be able to clearly state to their teen the following: (a) their deep concern and (b) their commitment to immediately intercede in every way necessary.

Waiting to act should not be an option. Interrupting the drug use behavior of an adult-child once they have moved out of the house, (including college), is very difficult. Therefore, every bit of energy aimed at intervening in their teen's drug behavior while they are still living at home is essential.

One of the non-so-obvious benefits of quickly and decisively intervening on a teen's drug use behavior, no matter how close they might be to heading off into the world (college or job) or how big or small the problem appears, is that **the teenager later in life will never be able to say that the issue of problematic drug use had not been raised.** When, at the age of 25, for example, the young adult gets a DUI, they won't be able to say "Wow, this is the first time I've had a problem with substances". This is important because drug abuse assessment relies on identifying patterns. A single event is not a pattern and can be written off as a fluke or bad luck. However, a pattern (two or more times) is more difficult to ignore.

Chapter 3
Talking isn't working, but is "rehab" really the next step?

Too many parents have found their teen in a residential treatment center or therapeutic boarding school without having had a fair shot at solving the problem at home. There are definitely cases where the teen is so out of control with their use and behavior that they need confinement and out-of-home-treatment over a sustained period of time. While many teens have greatly benefited from residential treatment, parents should however, be cautious not to pull that trigger too quickly.

Without a proper assessment conducted by an experienced clinician with expertise in adolescent substance use disorders, parents can easily find themselves overwhelmed and feeling compelled to act quickly. Some of these teens and families with earlier intervention may have been able to avoid the trauma, turmoil and expense of residential treatment. Therefore, and it bears repeating, finding a qualified adolescent therapist who can provide a thorough and thoughtful evaluation is imperative.

Treatment, What is it Good For?

The concept of treatment means different things to different people. Many parents think treating their teen's drug problem means one of two things; (a) intensive individual psychotherapy or (b) "rehab", with few other options. The next chapter outlines a number of treatment options, as well as when and how they should be used.

Yesterday, as I was writing this chapter, I got a call from a father concerned about his son's substance use. All the signs were there: decline in school performance, parents finding drugs, catching the boy getting high in his room late at night, anger and belligerence, new friends and more. The father said his son had been in counseling the year before for "behavior issues". The father went on to explain that the counseling wasn't helpful, that the therapist didn't think his son's pot use should be of concern and that his son didn't seem to like the therapist. This is a typical first call scenario including the "counseling didn't seem to work'" part. The father said I sounded like knowledgeable and hoped that I might be able to connect better with his son. I explained that I probably wouldn't end up being his son's "favorite guy", at least initially, and that instead a more effective approach would be to explore how he and his wife might work together to address their son's drug use. The father acknowledged that he and his wife had very different parenting styles and thought that that might be part of the problem. He said they had tried many approaches but nothing seemed to work.

The helplessness parents experience after trying many things without success can be crippling. When the three B's, bargaining, begging & berating don't work, parents often feel discouraged and out of options. By working with them directly to help them understand that, as parents (both positionally and functionally), they are *never* out of options, they are able to regain their confidence as effective parents and impact their teen's drug use in positive and decisive ways.

Chapter 4
The Treatment Continuum

There are basically six treatment options available to families.

1. Individual Psychotherapy
2. Family Therapy
3. Split Therapy Model
4. Benefit of the Doubt Intervention Model
5. Intensive Outpatient Treatment
6. Residential Treatment

These are ordered from least to most intensive and should match the severity of the problem.

Individual Psychotherapy

Individual therapy with substance using teens works best when it is done in conjunction with family therapy. This is discussed in the Split Therapy Model section below. It is questionable whether individual therapy with a teen who is actively using can be beneficial. There are many well-intentioned adolescent therapists who see teens who are using substances who have been successful in helping the teen to "use less" and/or quit. However, parents need to be very careful not to fall into the trap of assuming that, because their teen is going to therapy every week, the substance use/abuse issues are being addressed.

I have a rule in my practice: I never do individual therapy with a substance using teen. Below is a list of reasons why.

(1) I have never been successful in talking a teen into not using drugs.

(2) If the teen or parent tells me that the use is minimal, how does anyone know for sure? Drug testing (upcoming chapter) can not discern what a "little bit" or "I only use on the weekends" looks like.

(3) The effects of the substances makes the teen less "present", even when they are not obviously under the influence and therefore the therapy is less likely to "stick".

(4) I most often get referred cases where the teen is past the point where talk therapy might be helpful.

Split Therapy Model

The Split Therapy model delivers a great one- two punch, combining family therapy and individual therapy into a coordinated effort. In this model, one therapist sees the parents and teen while another therapist sees the teen alone. Unfortunately not all teens are candidates for individual therapy because most don't believe they have a problem. In these cases, often the only "problem" a teen can identify is that his/her parents are voicing concern and trying to prevent them from using drugs.

There are times, though, when a teen is willing and interested in being in therapy right from the beginning and in these cases parents should not hesitate to find an experienced adolescent therapist. If nothing else, the therapy provides a place for the teen to talk about what his/her parents are doing. The teen having their own therapist also allows the opportunity for the teen to identify what actions might be most beneficial (to the teen) relative to the work the parents are doing.

It is important to remember that the individual therapist's goal is not to talk the teen out of using drugs. The therapist's job is to help the teen to think about what they are doing to invite the intense unpleasant scrutiny they are experiencing from their parents and to identify and discuss what role drugs might be playing in their life.

Most families have tried some combination of family and/or individual therapy at some point prior to seeking help this time. These treatments may have been helpful to some extend but only for a time. The full extent of their teen's substance use, its amount, frequency and duration is easy to miss by even the most seasoned therapist but one who lacks substance abuse treatment experience. When family therapy is coordinated with the individual therapy the facts about the teen's substance abuse history more quickly bubble to the surface. There is some question, as information is exchanged back and forth between therapists, about whether the teen's confidentiality in the Split Therapy model may be compromised and whether, if the teen knows that the therapists are talking, they will be open and honest in their therapy. The line between creating and maintaining a solid therapeutic alliance with the teen and at the same time utilizing the information that ultimately will

22

* but does "the teen" want to think about what he's doing?

enhance the overall treatment can be thin. These are issues that the Split Therapy model treatment team needs to be constantly aware of. This balancing act is often difficult to manage and takes time and experience for therapists to develop.

Family Therapy

Family therapy offers the therapist a chance to see the parents and their teen in action and to assess the condition of the parent-child relationship. The fact that the teen is willing to participate, suggests they are still responsive, to some degree anyway, to their parents. It is also an opportunity to see if the drug use may be in reaction to parenting problems (i.e. over/under involvement, high parent conflict, verbal abuse, parent substance abuse, unreasonably high expectations, etc.). If any of these issues are present, it wouldn't excuse the teen's drug behavior, but it would suggest there are other important issues that may be contributing to the teen's drug use. In family therapy, these issues can be explored at the same time the teen's drug use is being addressed.

The Benefit of the Doubt

The Benefit of the Doubt strategy will be discussed in detail in the next chapter.

The Benefit of the Doubt is an approach I have developed over many years as a way to intervene in persistent adolescent substance use problems without having to resort to more intensive treatments. It is a strategy that falls somewhere between talk therapy (family and individual) and intensive outpatient treatment or residential treatment.

The Benefit of the Doubt approach has been used successfully in a broad range of family circumstances at varying stages of teenage drug use.

Intensive Outpatient Treatment (IOP)

Typically, intensive outpatient treatment is made up of a cluster of therapeutic components that, when brought together over a fairly short period of time (10 to 16 weeks with several contacts per week), can have a powerful impact, not just on the teen but on the parents as well.

For the past 30 years I have directed the **KIDS OFF CHEMICALS** *(kidsoffchemicals.com) intensive outpatient program that I founded in San Diego in 1987.*

The components of **KIDS OFF CHEMICALS** and most adolescent intensive outpatient programs are:

- Teen Recovery Group Therapy
- Family Therapy
- Multifamily Family Therapy
- Parent Coaching and Education
- Individual Therapy
- Drug Testing
- Recreational Outings

Most adolescent IOPs (Kids Off Chemicals included) are abstinence based, which means the goal of the treatment is for the teen to discontinue all substance use.

Residential Treatment

The term residential treatment describes a type of treatment in which the teen resides at a treatment facility for a period of time. Depending on the type of program, the teen may stay anywhere from a couple of weeks to 12-18 months.

The two types of out-of-home treatments that are used most, and often in tandem, are **therapeutic wilderness treatment** programs and **therapeutic boarding school** programs. A therapeutic wilderness treatment program stay is typically between 8 and 12 weeks. While there is quite a variation in how wilderness programs are structured, what they all have in common is an outdoor/ backpacking/nature emphasis. Teens spend anywhere from a couple of days at a time backpacking to preselected camp sites, to several weeks at a time without returning to basecamp.

In small groups of 4 - 8 teens, along with trained counselors with wilderness experience, teens learn self-reliance skills as well as how to cooperate in a group setting. These programs teach self-esteem enhancing skills such as learning to set fire by hand, rock climbing, cooking, cleaning, and other challenges that push the teen safely past their preconceived physical limits.

During the teen's stay they are regularly assessed by the clinical staff to determine if and when they might be ready to return home. If the clinical staff determines the teen *is* ready to return home directly from wilderness treatment, an aftercare plan is developed to help the teen and parents to continue to build on the progress made in treatment.

If the clinical staff determines, however, that the teen hasn't made the psychological and behavioral progress necessary for success at home, a recommendation is made for the teen's treatment to continue at a therapeutic boarding school program. It is estimated that between 60% and 80% of teens in wilderness programs move on to therapeutic boarding school treatment.

The lengths of stay at therapeutic boarding schools are typically between 10 and 18 months. Therapeutic boarding school programs are *not* wilderness based although many have wilderness components. Teens live in dorm-like environments, attend school, participate in regular individual and group counseling as well as weekly family therapy (phone or video chat) sessions with their parents.

Often the program recommends that the parents be in therapy while their teen is away at treatment. This work focuses on parenting issues that may have contributed to the teen's drug and behavioral problems and on developing strategies to solidify the gains the teen has made once he/she returns home.

The vast majority of teens referred to out-of-home placements have used substances to some extent.

Both treatment options address substance abuse problems either as the primary reason the teen required out-of-home treatment or as a behavior stemming from psychological concerns such as depression, trauma, family dysfunction, etc.

A more in-depth discussion concerning out-of-home adolescent treatment is beyond the scope of this book. If you have any questions about specific treatment programs, how to find quality treatment programs or how to match the type of program with a teen's needs, please contact me. You will find my contact information at the end of this book.

Chapter 5
The Benefit of the Doubt

The Benefit of the Doubt is an approach that teaches parents *not* to rush to conclude that because their teen has been using drugs and/or alcohol they necessarily have a substance use problem that requires treatment. It teaches parents how to give their teen the Benefit of the Doubt regarding their substance use. Innocent until proven guilty.

The parent's message is: "We will give you the Benefit of the Doubt that you don't have a drug and alcohol problem and that you *can* and *will* stop your substance use. We will assume this until we learn otherwise. Your job (son/daughter) is to demonstrate to us you don't have a substance use problem by stopping the use of all substances." The Benefit of the Doubt approach is a strategy that gives teens every opportunity to do this.

The Benefit of the Doubt approach is not a treatment protocol in the conventional sense. *It is a pre-treatment intervention approach that interrupts drug use behavior before more traditional treatment is needed.*

This chapter teaches parents (a) how to set up the Benefit of the Doubt strategy, (b) how to implement it, and (c) the importance of follow through.

In the adolescent treatment continuum, the Benefit of the Doubt strategy is designed to fit somewhere between outpatient therapy approaches (individual and/or family therapy) and the more intensive treatments such as Intensive Outpatient Treatment (IOP) and Residential Treatment options.

Over the past 10 years, the Benefit of the Doubt approach has been shaped, added to, and tweaked into what it is today. When using this approach, I consider myself more of a Parent Coach than a therapist. I direct, correct and guide parents as they learn and implement the strategy.

Most of this is done in face to face meetings. I also work by phone, video chat, email and/or text with families who live in other parts of the country. It is preferable, but not imperative, that the initial assessment and setup sessions be done in person. While this can represent the expense and inconvenience of travel, when weighed against the upheaval, disruption and trauma to families of sending their child to residential treatment, the trade-off is most often worth it.

*Contact information for setting up an assessment and a Benefit of the Doubt intervention can be found at the end of the book.

*Note to the reader: The term "drug" refers to all mind and mood altering substances INCLUDING alcohol.

Not every teen is a candidate for the *Benefit of the Doubt* approach.

It is important for parents to know that not every situation is appropriate for the Benefit of the Doubt approach. During the assessment it's important to note if any of the things listed below have occurred and if two or more of the these behaviors are present, the likelihood of the approach being successful decreases greatly. There seems to be a line of respect and decency that when crossed indicates a way of viewing and operating in the world that, while not insurmountable, requires more intensive and possibly more restrictive treatment.

- Violence toward parents/family members?
- Stolen money or other valuable belongings from parents/family members?
- Runaways from home lasting multiple days on multiple occasions?
- Not being affected by big takeaways? (driver's permits/licenses, electronics, etc.)
- Profane name calling on a consistent basis?
- Showing blatant disrespect for authority, police, principal, teachers, etc.?

The Benefit of the Doubt Approach in Action

The Initial Call

The initial call is important. This is when essential information is gathered to help discern whether the Benefit of the Doubt approach is appropriate for the family and teen. Below are some of the questions that are asked.

1. Does your son/daughter think they have a substance use problem? (90% of teens believe they do not)

2. Does your son/daughter know you are seeking help? If yes, how do they feel about it? If no, how do you think they *would* feel about it if they knew? Most teens, when they find out their parents are seeking help, say something like the following: "You're making a big deal over nothing" or "You're overreacting as usual" or " You're the one with the problem, get over yourself".

3. Do you think you'd be able to get your son/daughter to come in to the initial appointment with you? The answer to this question is telling and provides information about how engaged/disengaged the child is from his/her parents and their influence. When a teen can refuse a "request" by his/her parents to accompany them to a therapy appointment, it often reflects a situation where the parents have lost significant power and, potentially, control.

What's In It For Me?

Rule number one of human behavior: People never do anything unless there is some benefit to them. In the area of Motivational Psychology, there are no exceptions to this rule. As will be seen, the teen's motivation is a significant factor for success when the Benefit of the Doubt strategy is used.

As mentioned above, the initial assessment session may or may not include the teen. Ideally, though, the teen is present and parents are urged to do whatever it might take to have their teen attend. This may include promising lunch/dinner after or that the teen only has to attend one meeting. Aggressive coercion typically only invites resistance. If the teen steadfastly refuses, the parents are instructed to come alone.

When the teen *does* come to the initial session, their manner and attitude will say loudly and clearly how they feel about being there. Typically the teen is guarded, if not overtly resistant, but at least present. During these first sessions is when the teen may need some motivation to get onboard and this is done by helping them understand how they might benefit *by* participating. This session often goes something like this:

Me: "Your parents are bulldogs, they sound like they mean business in wanting you to stop getting high."

Teen: "Yeah"

Me: "Can you stop?"

Teen: "Yeah, I don't have a drug problem; I've told my parents that so many times."

At this point there is typically a pause and what is said next is important and is the foundation on which the Benefit of the Doubt approach is based:

Me: "You know, I don't get something here. You have your parents on your back constantly. And you hate that, right? The confusing part for me is that **you** *have invited them there. I don't get it. You are inviting the very thing that most teenagers hate; hovering, scrutinizing and judgmental parents. You know what I* *mean? You're a teenager. You should be out there having a bunch of fun, hanging out with your friends without your parents knowing or caring about every little thing you do. But that's not what you have. What you have are parents who are all over you. You have to admit that's a bit of a head scratcher; you're inviting the very thing you don't want.*

The good news is that there is a way to get them off your back. I can help you with that. The deal is, and you're probably way ahead of me on this, you have to stop using. You said a minute ago that you didn't have a drug problem, right? So quitting shouldn't be too hard.

Here's other side of the deal is that I guarantee we can get your parents off your back but here's kicker: You have to go first. If you stop using, my job will be to hold your parents' feet to the fire and get them to stop hovering. I can do that but not without your help.

You know drug testing will be a part of this, right? That's really the only way your parents will believe you've stopped. I know it's a weird thing to pee in a cup; do you have any friends who get drug tested?

Anyway, that's the deal; parents off your back guaranteed but you have to stop using. What do you think?"

Here, the teen finds him/herself in a bind. Their drug use behavior invites exactly the kind of invasive attention teens detest. From a developmental perspective, the period of adolescence is about teens separating psychologically from their parents. While not a conscious process, their goal is to experience being in the world independent of their parents. This process is called individuation and is essential for psychological growth. The last thing in the world a teen wants is to have hovering parents, which is essentially why this technique works. Upwards of 90% of the time the teen accepts the plan. That doesn't mean it's clear sailing but what it does represent for the teen is an initial shift in thinking, all resulting from the teen understanding how he/she might benefit from the process.

The 85% Rule

There is metric that predicts the probability of behavior change in humans. When people consciously execute a new behavior, when there is an opportunity to do either the new desired behavior or default to the old undesired behavior, at least 85% of the time over a period of time, the new behavior will be more easily and efficiently reproduced in the future. On the other hand, executed behavior falling below 85% will most likely fail to reliably produce any new, long-lasting behavior.

In other words, when a person practices a new behavior, they tend to get better at it.

This principle applies to parenting. When parents consistently follow the set of guidelines in the Benefit of the Doubt strategy, at least 85% of the time, change will occur in the family system.

Give It Time to Work

Patience and consistency while using the Benefit of the Doubt approach (85% rule) is essential. Initially, parents may have success trying new things to influence their teen's drug use behavior, but over time the strategy, whatever it might be, often reaches a point of diminishing returns. This typically has more to do with parent inconsistency than with a faulty strategy.

Several months back I had a family in my office who had tried multiple strategies. These parents were eager learners who had researched many of the the newest approaches to get their teen to stop using drugs and had read many parenting self-help books.

I commented, "It sounds like you have tried a lot of things to help your daughter."

The daughter, sitting next to me in a chair, (the parents were sitting together on the couch), testily replied "yeah it's like I'm the guinea pig for their next experiment. They don't get it, none of that crap is going to work."

I turned to parents and asked, "What happens when you implement a new plan?"

The father returned, "Nothing. we usually stop because they never seem to work, and believe me we have tried."

These were well-intentioned parents, worried to death that their daughter would eventually put herself in a harmful situation. However, they were discouraged and exhausted.

Parenting Rule: Don't give up. As mentioned above, when strategies don't work, it's typically not the fault of the strategy. It's more likely that the parents don't give it enough of a chance. When something (anything) new is applied to a situation there will be push back.

An example of this is the human body. When a person decides to get in shape and go to the gym, the first 2 to 3 weeks can be very uncomfortable. Essentially the body is saying "I like the status quo and don't want to give it up." The initial discomfort, along with *no noticeable results* causes the person to relent and stop working out. Health clubs make a fortune from abandoned New Year's resolutions. However, if the person sticks it out, gets over the hump of the first 2 to 3 weeks of soreness, the payoffs begin to justify the pain.

So it goes for parents trying to intervene in their teen's drug behavior. The teen *will* push back, often vehemently at first. They have seen their parent's ill-conceived efforts before and will wait it out, thinking that if they throw a wrench or two in the works, their parents will abandoned the new plan as they have all the others in the past. And when they do, the teen's resistance is rewarded. Emboldened by their success, the teen is ready to defeat the next strategy when it comes along.

Once parents have initiated the Benefit of the Doubt approach, they should NEVER abandon the strategy.

A few tweaks here and there are expected, but the fundamental plan needs consistent adherence.

Once the teen sees that their parents are committed to the plan, in relatively short order, things will start to change. Parents need to remember it is their job to convince their teen that they mean business though. Their teen won't be a believer initially but the parent's *consistent actions, over time,* will be the difference between old strategies that have failed and the eventual success of the Benefit of the Doubt.

There is a story about a farmer and his donkey. The farmer had great confidence that his donkey would always do whatever he asked of it. A passer-by, upon hearing the claim, asked the farmer to demonstrate. Accepting the challenge, the farmer pulled out a 2x4 and clobbered the donkey between the eyes. Appalled and confused, the passer-by cried, "I thought you said the donkey would do whatever you asked" The farmer replied easily, "He will, but I have to get his attention first."

This story illustrates the central problem parent's face when attempting to intervene in their teen's substance abuse behavior; *they don't have their child's attention.* The parents have been ignored and placated and the three B's that parents typically use, begging, bargaining and berating aren't working. It's not until the parents get their teen's attention that things start to change.

Leverage & Consequences

By the time most parents seek help, they are worn out, discouraged and desperate. They have tried all the things they can think of, including entertaining some questionable advice from well-meaning friends and family. Everyone, it seems, has an opinion about how to manage a wayward teen; Send him to a boot camp or to a military school or to the kind, but ill-equipped aunt and uncle with a farm in Oklahoma; "They'll put him to work, it'll do him good . . . he won't have time to get high." The parents feel as though they've lost control of their teen and, often times, they have. Helping parents regain their parenting power centers around giving consequences for unwanted behavior. Some parents wonder why they can't just reward positive behavior instead of punishing negative behavior. Parents are actually encouraged to do both. When their teen does well in school, praise them or/and reward them. However, substance abuse behavior typically does not discernibly decrease when only rewarding positive behavior. A dinner out for a good grade will not have much impact on whether the teen smokes pot tomorrow. Therefore, the biggest impact on teen drug behavior is typically consequences that focus on take-aways.

Choosing Consequences

When choosing and implementing consequences, here are the guidelines:

1. Parents should NEVER implement a consequence when they are angry. Often, in those circumstances, the consequence leveled will be inappropriate, too long in duration and unenforceable. Parents should take time to calm down (which sometimes can be hours) and discuss consequence options with the other parent or a close friend who is in the know regarding the overall plan. Waiting does two things. First, it produces a consequence appropriate to the violation and second, it allows the teen time to contemplate his/her fate. With a measured tone and well-chosen words (tough to do when upset), the parent's response to the violation might go something like this: "It's really unfortunate you chose to... (fill in the blank). There will be a consequence coming but I/we are not ready to disclose what it is. I/we will let you know in several hours (or tomorrow, if the infraction occurred at night) what it will be."

2. Parents should never ask the teen what they think an appropriate consequence should be. It rarely produces anything of value and often ends up in another conflict.

3. When choosing a consequence, parents should use the following rule of thumb:

AN EFFECTIVE CONSEQUENCE IS THE TAKING AWAY OF ANYTHING THAT IS IMPORTANT TO THE TEEN OVER WHICH THE PARENTS STILL HAVE CONTROL.

Parents should not take away a skateboard that hasn't been used in a year because it will not have an impact. It doesn't represent something of value to the teen. Cell phones, computers and driving privileges tend to be the most attention-getting options. There is an important exception to this guideline. Parents should not leverage or consequence their teen by taking away self-esteem enhancing activities. This includes but is not limited to: sports; playing, practicing or performing music; participating in acting/theater or involvement in art. It is important to have these kinds of activities and interests in a teen's life because they help them feel good about themselves (a dad forcing his son to play football if the son clearly doesn't want to doesn't count). It's been shown that when a teen participates in one or more of these self-esteem enhancing activities, the prognosis for recovery from a substance abuse problem improves. This is because they have something that's important to them to go *back to* once they are longer using substances. It's very difficult to engineer this into a teen's life if it's not already there.

4. Once implemented, a consequence should not last longer than 7 to 10 days. There are several reasons for this: a) After 7 to 10 days the effectiveness of the consequence starts to diminish (the point of the consequence is to get and keep the teen's attention). b) Long consequences eventually become a burden

to the parents, often to the point where the parents abandon them just to be freed from the hassle. c) To prevent running out of consequences. If parents "spend" their most potent consequences (i.e. cell phone take-away) and that consequence is tied up for a couple of months, they can't use it again until it's available. At that point, parents are forced to use second tier consequences (i.e. rides) which may not be quite as effective.

5. Identify the day, and even the time of day the consequence will start and stop. Parents must commit to not deviate from the plan, no matter how "good" their teen's behavior is. It's amazing how much trash a teen can take out, without being asked, during this time!

6. Fortunately, there are consequences that naturally exist in the world and whenever possible, parents should use them. The concept is called *Concentric Circles of Consequences.* Think of it as circles inside circles where the teen is represented as a dot in the middle of the smallest circle. Each circle represents a system that naturally has influence over the teen. The smallest circle represents the influence of parents. The next circle out represents things like school, sports etc. The next circle out represents more "real" world influences like having a job. The next circle represents the influence of the legal system, in a teen's case, the Juvenile Justice System. An example is when a teen doesn't go to school, the school responds by lowering grades. If the teen continues to be truant he/she may not pass and eventually may

not graduate. These are the natural consequences of not going to school.

Other examples might be when a teen doesn't go to work, they may lose their job. If the teen violates the law, the legal system will step in.

It can be very difficult for parents to stand by and watch while their teen fails a class, or loses a job or gets arrested. Parents need to restrain themselves and resist the urge to rescue their teen. The parental instinct is to protect their child from harm. When parents take a step back, however, they hopefully can see that "the way of the world" provides lessons, sometimes very tough lessons, which may not be gotten any other way.

Parents Talk Too Much

Some time back, a father and daughter came in to see me. The presenting problem was that the girl was defiant, using drugs and putting herself in dangerous social situations. As the assessment session proceeded, the father dominated more and more of the discussion. He would look at me at the beginning of each tirade and then quickly turn to his daughter. Each time his daughter slumped further into her chair.

The father said essentially the same thing each time he talked: "These are the reasons drugs are bad for you: if you keep using drugs and running around with bad kids your life will be ruined; you know drug addiction runs in our family so you should know better."

At one point I turned to the daughter and asked her if she had heard any of this before. She said "Are you kidding? Every day. I know the speech before it comes out of his mouth. He thinks it makes a difference, like at some point I'm going to say 'Gee dad, sure glad you told me that for the 400th time. I just got it, thanks!'"

And so it goes for most kids and their parents. It's hard to blame parents for lecturing because it's often all they feel they can do but it is rarely helpful and often causes the teen to *stop* listening, resulting in the exact opposite of the what the parents are hoping for.

Once the Benefit of the Doubt approach is implemented, there should be no talk at all about the teen's drug use. The strategy is in place and the parents and teen understand the expectations and the consequences if the expectations are not met. In essence then, the strategy does its own talking which frees up the parents and their son/daughter to, potentially, have conversations about other things; things that potentially *connect* rather than *divide*.

Chapter 6
Drug Testing & Implementing the Benefit of the Doubt

Parents don't have babies so that one day they can drug test them yet drug testing is an essential component in the Benefit of the Doubt approach (just as it is for most other treatment strategies). Without it, the approach won't work.

Like it or not, drug using teens are better at hiding their drug use than parents are at detecting it. When families are in the midst of their teen's drug using chaos, most of the conflicts center around whether parents think their teen is currently or has been high. "You're high; no I'm not, yes you are, no I'm not" is how the back and forth usually goes. Parents try to become drug sleuths. They smell breath, look at eyes, listen to speech, and watch movements in order to discover whether their teen is high or drunk, all the while thinking they are better at it than they actually are. Unfortunately, these cat and mouse interaction patterns do nothing but drive a wedge more deeply between the parents and their teen.

There is a saying: "To be a good drug user, you need to be a good liar; otherwise your drug-using career will be short".

Drug testing takes the guess work out of knowing whether a teen is using drugs or not.

Getting Started with Drug Testing

There are many ways to test for drugs. In the vast majority of cases urine is used to test for substances and breathalyzers are used to specifically test for alcohol. Below is an overview of what tests are used, how to administer a drug test and reasons why drug testing is important.

When and How Often

Urine should be collected on a *random* testing schedule. Teens who are used to being tested may figure out that if testing tends to be every other Thursday, for instance, then a hit of cannabis right after being tested might not be detected two weeks later (more on how long drugs are detectable in urine below). Randomizing the testing schedule eliminates this concern. A frequent question is how often should parents test their teen. Four to six times per month is typically adequate. To some this may not sound frequent enough, however, because the tests are administered randomly, in the teen's mind, the next test could be at any time. Therefore, a randomized test schedule can reduce how often the testing needs to be done.

In addition to randomization, using events or circumstances to help determine when to test can be helpful. For instance, if the teen went to a concert the night before or stayed overnight at a friend's, it might be a good time to test. If the teen looks odd, sleepy, has dilated pupils or slow or slurred speech, it may be worth a test.

Reading the signs, events during the week and using a random testing schedule are the ingredients for a reliable testing strategy.

How To Collect Urine

The actual collection of the urine is one of the most important, if not *the* most important, parts of testing for drugs. Parents need to be sure that the urine they are testing comes out of their teen's body.

Urine upon Request Guidelines

The following two guidelines are put into place at the outset of implementing the Benefit of the Doubt approach:

1. The teen will provide a urine sample when asked.

2. Refusal to provide a urine sample will be responded to as if the sample was positive for substances.

There are only two reasons a teen wouldn't provide a sample; first, he/she has something to hide, meaning they had used and knew it would be discovered. And second, if they were *unable* to urinate when asked; "I can't pee" or "I just went." This may be true, however, it is sometimes used to avoid the fact that their urine will show positive for drugs. When/if the teen says they aren't able to urinate, parents should have them drink a 12 ounce glass of water. Most people will be able to produce some urine 20 minutes later. During that time, it is important to have the teen remain within sight because there are times when this is a stall tactic in order to put together a fake sample. When parents aren't vigilant, their child may miraculously appear with a cup of urine in their hand and say "Here, I ended up being able to pee after all." The problem, of course, is that the sample collection wasn't observed and there is no way to know what's truly in the cup. It could be someone else's urine, contaminated urinate, fake urine, water, etc...

Door Jamb Collection Method

In order to ensure that parents are collecting *their* teen's urine and to avoid any of the faking methods described in the next section, parents are advised to use the "door jamb method."

This is where the teen is in the bathroom and the parent stands, with the bathroom door open, in the door way facing the opposite side of the door jamb. This allows the parent to observe adequately with their peripheral vision that their teen is urinating into the specimen cup. No dipping into the toilet, no use of the faucet, no adding something to the urine. Once the urine is in the container and handed to the parent, it should be warm and look and smell like urine. From there the parent can test the sample with confidence that the results belong to their teen.

Beating The Test

The lengths to which teens (adults too) will go to beat a drug test, especially when the stakes are high, can be mind boggling. Parents need to be vigilant and consistent with their collection method in order to be able to trust the test results.

Detoxifiers

Many smoke shops, head shops and vape shops sell detoxifiers that are designed to rid the body of substances. Whether these detoxifiers actually work is debatable. Nonetheless, teens usually don't have the money nor are they organized well enough to make consistent use of these. Additionally, as discussed previously, how and when parents collect the urine will neutralize the possible use of detoxifiers.

Tubes, Tape and a Bag

Several years ago, some parents presented with the following story. Their teen was clearly using substances but all the drugs tests were negative. The parents were collecting the urine correctly (the door jamb method) but something was amiss.

At one point the parents were instructed to ask their son to remove his shirt prior to urinating. With hesitance he did so, revealing a fairly elaborate contraption made of surgical tubing running from a small IV-like bag, which contained the urine, taped just below his armpit. The tubing ran down into his pants then into his crotch with a clamp on the end. When he was asked to urinate he simply pulled the tubing slightly through his pant zipper, just enough so that his parents couldn't see, loosened the clamp slightly and deposited someone else's urine into the cup. This represented a great deal of preparation and was only possible because the parents let their son know in advance when he would be tested. Once the parents started randomly collecting their son's urine the test results began showing positive.

The "Whizzinator"

Another method to deliver some else's urine into the specimen cup is the use of a fake penis. The "Whizzinator" is one of many fake penis options found on the internet. The fake penis, which holds someone else's or synthetic urine, is kept in the boy's crotch area to keep it at body temperature. The fake penis is then squeezed to release the urine into the cup. This is easier to pull off than the surgical tube method and has the added feature of looking realistic in case the parents happened to look closely.

"Popping the Bottle"

For girls desperate to pass a drug test, this is a method known as, among other names, "popping the bottle." Again some preparation is required which can be neutralized by a random and unannounced testing strategy. Girls put either synthetic or someone else's urine in a small bottle with a lid that's easy to open and then insert it into their vagina prior to testing. Holding the specimen cup under her while sitting on the toilet, the girl opens the bottle so that urine from the bottle pours into the specimen cup.

Synthetic Urine

Synthetic urine can be bought online and will produce negative test results for both home tests as well as lab tests. It is not possible for labs or home testing kits to detect if urine is synthetic or not.

Testing for different substances

Alcohol

Relying on the use of urine to detect alcohol, even if the detection instrument being used tests for alcohol, is not advised. Alcohol is metabolized and eliminated from the body very quickly (water soluble) and is therefore difficult to detect in real time. How long alcohol is detectable in the body depends on how much is consumed and ranges between 4 to 15 hours. Therefore, the most efficient way to detect alcohol is by using a breathalyzer which can be purchased online for $80-120. Testing for alcohol should be more frequent than the 4 to 6 times per month, stated previously, because of how quickly alcohol is processed through body. Due to the obvious safety issues, increased testing frequency is especially important if the teen is driving.

Cannabis

Using urine to test for cannabis (marijuana), on the other hand, is very reliable and efficient. Because cannabis is stored in the fat cells (fat soluble) the detection time period is longer than water soluble drugs (see below). Twenty- five days (+/-) is the typical "wash out" period for THC (the psychoactive ingredient in cannabis). This is based on consistent drug use, 3 to 5 times per week over a period of 6 months or more. For less consistent and less frequent use and for single-use relapses, the wash out period may be shorter.

Because cannabis stays in the body longer and can therefore can be detected for a longer period of time, testing is a little more involved. The amount of THC can be quantified (or measured) in the body to obtain a baseline amount. Each successive test (usually spaced 7 to 10 days apart) is then compared to the baseline to see whether the amount goes up or down. If the levels go down relative to the baseline, it indicates no drug use. If the levels stay the same as baseline or go up, it indicates drug use. It is important to use this method in order to avoid getting to the end of the wash out period (25 days +/-) only to still have a positive test. This would indicate the teen had been using all the while and thereby delaying the intervention work by 25 days.

Water Soluble Drugs

Water soluble drugs, which include opioids, cocaine, amphetamines and others, have a detection time period of approximately 2 to 4 days following use. Therefore, increased testing frequency may be necessary for these drugs, at least initially.

An exception to the 2 to 4 day wash out rule for water soluble drugs is benzodiazepines (Ativan, Xanax, etc). When benzodiazepines are taken consistently over a 6 month period (+/-), they may be detectable for up to 2 weeks and in some cases longer.

False Positives

False positives (when there has been no drug use but the drug test detects substances) do happen, but very rarely. The dip stick drug tests found online or at drug stores are very reliable and are on par with lab tests. When a test is "inexplicably" positive, there is often a story which accompanies the positive result where the teen passionately swears he/she didn't use. "I was in a room where a bunch of people were getting high so the test is showing a contact high." or "It must be residual from when I *was* getting high." or "How could I have gotten high, I've been with you 24 hours a day for the past forever," and so on. In time, these fables are often admitted to and the family moves on.

If there are serious questions about the validity of a test result, another test should be given immediately. If drug use is occurring and parents get snookered once, or even twice by a creative story, consistent drug testing will eventually reveal the truth.

GREEN FLAG MEETING:
READY, SET, GO

The Green Flag Meeting represents the culmination of all the preparation the parents have done up to this point. This is the time when the parents sit down with their teen to outline the Benefit of the Doubt strategy and begin implementation.

The Green Flag Meeting should be brief and to the point. The parents essentially explain their plan regarding intervening in their teen's drug use behavior. It often goes something like this:

"Thanks for being willing to sit down with us. As you know we are very concerned about your substance use so we have come up with a plan that we want to share with you."

Assuming the teen is willing to sit down in the first place (not always the case) and hasn't bolted from the room, the parents should proceed.

The next step is to hand them a copy of the:

5 Rules

- No use of any mind or mood altering substances
- No friends in the house without parent permission
- Attending school is mandatory
- "Where a-bouts known" at all times and curfew adhered to (determined by parents)
- No violence, property damage or threat of either.

For most families, some of these rules are already in place or may not be of concern. The most important thing to note, however, is that all five rules have one thing in common. They are all <u>measurable</u> (they either happened or they didn't; no gray area) which reduces arguments and conflicting interpretations about whether the rule was violated or not. For that reason, *not* on the list are things like:

- Keep your room clean (conflict: clean by whose standard?)

- Exercise (conflict: what constitutes exercise?)
- No cursing (conflict: is "damn" ok? What about "sh*t?")

Parents continue:

*"We will be doing drug testing starting today. We know that because you have been using, your first test may come back positive. We won't consider that a violation (rule #1) but the second test needs to be negative (review the **testing for cannabis** section above) or we are left to assume you have continued to use."*

At this point the parents ask their teen to provide a urine sample. Parents explain (if using a lab) that the results will be back in 3 to 5 days. If using a home testing kit (not advised at this stage because a quantified baseline for THC is necessary and home kits only provide detected or undetected results) the results can be gotten in about 3 minutes.

Important: Parents should *not* tell their teen what substances they are testing for. If they know, teens will sometimes use a drug that isn't being tested for, even if it's not one that has been used ordinarily. Parents can and should let their teen know that they will be tested for alcohol by way of a breathalyzer.

Next, parents explain the consequences (see section above on consequences):

"Because of how strongly we feel about you not using drugs, we are prepared to go to any lengths to see that that stops. This means that if we aren't successful

in accomplishing it by using the Benefit of the Doubt approach (it's ok for parents to name the strategy) we will be looking to intensify our efforts, which may include intensive outpatient treatment and/or residential treatment. We are very, very hopeful that it won't come to that but we want you to know how serious we are."

Here, some parents may feel like they are issuing a threat. Instead, parents are encouraged to see it as:

1. Motivation for their teen to stop using substances.

2. A clear statement about the parent's resolve to intervene.

3. Parent's commitment to a well thought out strategy.

Finally, parents ask if their teen has any questions. Questions for clarification sake are perfectly fine. Questions to bait parents into an argument are not acknowledged. Parents need to be on their toes at this point to cover the specifics of the strategy (it's a good idea for parents to have them written down and have the list handy) and keep it short. If the meeting goes on for more than 10 minutes, it usually means there is some baiting or negotiation going on. There is no negotiation here. The strategy should stand as stated.

As discussed earlier, it is at this point that parents essentially *stop talking to their teen about their drug use*. Let the plan do the talking. Talk about something else; sports, the weather, politics, but not drug use. They need to trust the strategy.

Once the green flag has dropped, things often calm down a bit and the mood in the house improves. This is typically only true if the teen has bought into the strategy and plans to cooperate. For teens who have not, the tide may not turn right away and parents need to be patient and persevere.

During this time family counseling and/or individual counseling should continue. For the teen, having the support of therapy can be very helpful.

The First Drug Test Results

If the teen's drug of choice is cannabis, it is recommended that the parents use a lab to analyze the urine in order to measure the amount of THC. The first test, as discussed in a previous section, will typically be positive for cannabis and possibly for water soluble drugs as well if taken within the previous 2 to 4 days.

It bears repeating that because the parent's strategy has only just been implemented, it is expected that there will be substances in the teen's system. Teens should not receive consequences for these first results. The second drug test result are the one of most concern.

Cannabis Testing Review: If the second test result shows that the THC level has not gone down relative to the baseline, parents are left to conclude that there has been cannabis use and parents will need to discuss their response options. If the results are negative and/or the level of THC has gone down, it indicates that the teen has accepted the strategy (at least for now). This is good news and parents should congratulate their son/daughter on a job well done.

Important: When the second drug test is negative for all substances and THC level has gone down, too often parents fail to recognize this as a victory or acknowledge how difficult this might have been for their teen. Instead of congratulations, parents make the mistake of saying:

"Well yeah, not using drugs is what we expected all along. I don't think congratulating you for something that was expected to begin with is necessary."

For a teen to hear this after going from using drugs one day to not using the next, is demoralizing and counterproductive. Instead, parents need to verbally acknowledge the results, praise their teen for their achievement and then possibly invite a conversation with them about how they feel about what they've accomplished. It is important for parents to look for opportunities to be positive. Engaging their teen with "how do *you* feel about...." type questions is a way to set a new tone for interacting.

Recharge Defined; Review, Consequence and Continue

In the following sections the term *recharge* will be used to describe an option available to parents following a positive drug test result. A *recharge* involves parents reviewing the infraction, consequencing the infraction and continuing with the Benefit of the Doubt strategy. A *recharge* gives their teen another chance (Benefit of the Doubt) to show that he/she doesn't have a drug problem.

Second Drug Test: Scenarios That Could Explain a Positive Result

While not a good sign that the second drug test is positive (or the same or greater amount of THC in cannabis tracking), it's not the end of the world either. A positive test can indicate a number of different things.

Below are the various scenarios that typically explain a positive second test.

1. Last hoorah.

2. Wrong place, wrong time, wrong people.

3. "Screw you"

4. Bona fide substance use disorder.

Each scenario is discussed below in addition to parents' response options.

1. **Last hoorah:** A last hoorah is in essence a goodbye and in this case a goodbye to drug use. While not an ideal start, this typically warrants a *recharge* (review, consequence and continue) by the parents. Remember the parent's job is to convince their teen that they, the parents, are committed to the strategy and the message to the teen, therefore, needs to be that they just used their one "get out jail free card."

2. **Wrong place:** It's important to remember that all of the teen's friends, his/her routine (before and after school) and the desire to get high are all still present even though the green flag has been dropped. Parents should closely evaluate the kind of response their teen has to the news that their drug test results were positive. If the teen's response looks like sincere remorse and contrition, that's a good sign. However, if the response has a "no big deal" sentiment, parents should be concerned. Reading and interpreting the response can be tricky. Most often, at this juncture though, *re-charging* the plan is warranted but with a convincing warning from the parents that there will be no more chances.

3. **"Screw you!"** This scenario means typically "I think this plan sucks and I'm not going to stop getting high." *Recharging* the plan following this kind of response should only be done after careful consideration. The teen is saying loudly and clearly that he/she has no intention to stop using substances so a *recharge* may be just delaying the inevitability of the need for more intensive treatment.

It's important for parents to remember that this scenario does not necessarily indicate a budding substance use disorder (although it may lead to one) and therefore needs to be distinguished from a bona fide substance use disorder (#4 below). The "Screw You!" scenario is typically more about anger and family dysfunction than a substance use disorder. It often represents a hostile power struggle between the teen and his/her parents. This is an unfortunate and complicated dynamic because there are many others ways for teens to express anger and hostility toward their parents. Using drugs, while attention-getting, is an ineffective method for the teen to be heard and taken seriously (not that teen rebellion is ever necessarily a well thought out endeavor). In time, once the drug use stops, the family may be able to address, in family therapy, some of the issues that underlie the teen's anger and hostility.

In the "screw you" scenario, the parents need to respond by giving their teen consequences that have the greatest chance of getting his/her attention (see the section below on Consequencing Positive Drug tests).

4. **Bona Fide Substance Use Disorder:** This scenario is fairly rare, occurring in only about 12 to 15% of cases. Because teens have only been in the world for a relatively short period of time, physiological and/or psychological reliance on a substance has not yet had a chance to take full root. In most cases and with most substances, it takes time to develop an addiction. In view of this fact, most teen use is due to a combination of poor judgment, impulsivity, social pressures, curiosity and rebellion. This dangerous mix of dynamics can certainly *lead* to a substance use disorder, but this is typically not the case.

In the case of a *true* bona fide substance use disorder, when news of a second positive drug test elicits resignation, bewilderment and confusion on the part of the teen about his/her behavior, it should tip off parents to wonder about their teen's true ability to stop using drugs. In the face of what their teen stands to lose by continuing to use drugs, the question about whether the "choice" to use still exists is important. This doesn't mean that the parents shouldn't issue consequence and *recharge* the plan. It is, however, an indication that the parents should begin researching residential treatment programs that specialize in the treatment of substance use disorders.

Giving Consequences For Positive Drug Results

In response to a second positive test, consequences & leverage need to be put into action. In a previous section (Leverage and Consequences) some important details of consequencing, including how and under what circumstances they should be given out were outlined. When there is a second positive drug test, it is important to know, specifically, *what* to leverage. First, the parents need to remind themselves **"what are those things that are important to my teen over which I still have control?"**

Important: When the teen is of driving age and/or is already driving, restricting or delaying him/her from obtaining a permit or license, or limiting driving privileges, typically **last longer than 7 to 10 days**. *Because of the danger and liability associated with driving a car,* **3 to 6 months, along with consistent clean drug tests, is typically the length of time of the consequence.** *It makes sense that properly* *operating a 3000 pound vehicle requires a substance free brain!*

(See chapter 5 to review details regarding consequences and leverage.)

Use *Recharge* Wisely

As we discussed above, a second positive drug test scenario comes with a *recharge* option. Just like the boy who cried wolf however, it is important for parents to understand that the *recharge* option should be used only after careful thought. *Recharge* can reasonably be used once, maybe twice, but in rare cases, three times. Too many *recharges* makes the parents look ambivalent and weak and gives the teen conflicting messages about their parents commitment to the plan.

Fork in the Road

After a second positive drug test, many parents become discouraged. Some begin to wonder whether their teen can be reached. This represents a time of tough decisions, a fork in the road. One fork says "Let's stay with the Benefit of the Doubt approach and see if things turn around." The other fork points in the opposite direction: "We've seen enough. It's time to move to more intensive treatment." The following sections unpacks both decisions and their ramifications.

The Final *Recharge*

Most parents decide to *recharge (*i.e. go one more round of drug testing and give their teen the Benefit of the Doubt one last time) and hope it works. And it often does. It is at this point that teens who haven't bought into the Benefit of the Doubt approach previously, come to terms with the reality of what they stand to lose if they continue to use. Most teens realize that it's not just their cell phone that might be taken away and that the stakes are higher. Instead they begin to understand that their parent's next move might be to send them to a residential treatment program. Parents should continue to view the intensification of treatment as a means to provide their teen the *help* they need. Most teens, however, won't see it that way and instead, regard it as *punishment.* Parents should never bring up residential treatment as an option unless they are willing to follow through with it. However, once broached, it can be a very potent attention-getter and can turn a teen's ambivalence into compliance in a short period of time.

If the message: "You need to stop using substances" *has* gotten through, evidenced by the second drug test being negative, it is an indication that the teen has made the decision to stop their drug use and, therefore, more negative drug test results should start rolling in.

**This is what the parents have been waiting for but it's not yet time to celebrate. However a fist pump and an audible "YES!" are permitted.

In this phase of the strategy is where some of the biggest relationship changes take place. It is also the phase where the teen starts to generally function better as the effects of the substances begin to diminish. Often the teen's grades improve somewhat, a more consistent mood may be observed (parents need to remember that they are still dealing with an adolescent who, even without substances, would be challenged by mood swings), as well as noticeably less conflict at home.

To capitalize on these gains and to identify new ways for the teen to operate in the world without drugs and alcohol, family and individual therapy should continue. Many teens have never had the opportunity to have fun without being high or drunk and it takes time for them to figure out how to do this. Therapy can help with this.

I had a 17 year old girl once tell me that the things other kids seemed to enjoy were really boring, if not tedious, for her. She had been using drugs and alcohol since she was 13 and the only sober fun she'd experienced was before she started using drugs. She considered that "little kid fun." This meant all the fun she had had since the age of 13 was while she was high.

Don't Make This Mistake

Parents have to be very careful at this juncture to not rest on their laurels and forget that this new order of things takes constant vigilance and that new patterns take time to take hold. Patience and consistency is called for as well as a commitment to continued drug testing.

I got a call some time back from a mother I had seen (with her son) in my office a year before. She described how well she and her son had done in the months following our work together but how, recently, things had begun to slip. In the areas parents generally focus on -grades, attitudes and behaviors- the mother was concerned her son was almost all the way back to where he was when she first sought help. My first concern when I get calls like this is whether or not drug testing is still being administered. This mother sheepishly admitted she had stopped because things were going so well.

Often, one of the reasons things go so well following an intervention like the Benefit of the Doubt, is *because* parents continue to drug test. In the above case, the mother's son had no doubt noticed that drug testing had stopped, creating an opening for all the old temptations and opportunities, which were still

65

there begging for his attention, to trigger a relapse. In demonstration of this point, many teens ask their parents to continue to drug test them when it's become clear the parents have slacked off. What the teen is psychologically needing is the security that comes from limits and structure. The main psychological dilemma in adolescent development is *autonomy versus dependence.* There is a constant tension between righteously demanding freedom and being freaked out that the world is too complicated to figure out.

The art of parenting a teen is finding the sweet spot between too much and too little structure. The art of parenting a substance abusing teen is even trickier. Continuing drug testing, even after the initial crisis quiets down, is part of the art.

We've Seen Enough

If the third test is positive for substances then decisive action is called for. The parents have used up their reasonable allotment of *recharges* and it's time to modify the plan.

Every parent hopes that the Benefit of the Doubt approach would have been successful by now and are often discouraged and disappointed. And yet, however painful, it is important for parents to review the issues that led them to intervene in the first place and how, in spite of all the opportunities afforded their teen to stop using drugs and, in spite of all the negative consequences they would face if they decided not to stop, they *chose to continue using drugs nonetheless*. At this point it's difficult to deny that their teen's substance abuse problem may be more entrenched and advanced than initially thought.

To intensify the treatment and move toward an approach other than the Benefit of the Doubt, parent's will often consider more conventional treatment such as intensive outpatient or residential treatment. Intensive outpatient treatment (IOP) definitely has its place in the treatment continuum, however, at this juncture it may lack the firepower to turn things around and therefore residential treatment is more often the next step. These are tough decisions for parents. The residential treatment option can be expensive, disruptive to the family and emotionally traumatic to all involved but, at the same time, often necessary to appropriately treat their teen's substance use disorder.

Last Last Chance

There are parents who will decide not to go another round. They have seen enough and are convinced that their teen has dug in and decided to continue using drugs. Yet some parents, before considering residential treatment, decide to give their teen one more chance. At this important juncture, parents are coached to be sure that what they are offering is truly their teen's *last last* chance. Otherwise, parents run the risk of looking like they are defaulting to their old ways (all talk and no action). There are times when one more chance is what the teen needs in order to get the message, however, there are other times when a *last last* chance is merely putting off the inevitable. Either way parents are encouraged to begin researching residential treatment programs.

Conclusion

Parenting a teen is a difficult and at times daunting undertaking. Parenting a teen who is abusing drugs and alcohol can make this process even more complicated, exhausting and, at times, terrifying. The overall purpose of this book has been to educate parents in the things relevant to their teen's substance use as well as acquainting them with the Benefit Of the Doubt intervention model.

Over the years, the Benefit of the Doubt approach has been used successfully to interrupt the substance use cycle in many families. This early intervention/pre-treatment strategy has often succeeded where conventional talk therapies have failed. Other treatment approaches (therapy, intensive outpatient and residential treatment) have their place on the menu of treatment options and are effective and necessary under certain circumstances. However the Benefit of the Doubt approach represents an alternative that often make more intensive, expensive and disruptive approaches unnecessary.

The parenting mantra, "Kids don't come with manuals," rings uncomfortably true for many parents. In the world of parenting teenagers with substance abuse problems, the Benefit of the Doubt approach may be the closest thing we have to that manual.

About the author

Dr. Mark Falls has worked in the field of psychology for over 30 years. In 1985, he founded KIDS OFF CHEMICALS, an Intensive Outpatient Program for substance abusing adolescents and their families.

Dr. Falls is licensed both as a clinical psychologist and as a Marriage and Family Therapist. In his free time he enjoys sports of all kinds and building things. Dr. Falls is the father of four children, all of whom have survived adolescence. He lives and practices in Santa Rosa, Ca.

To obtain more information or set-up an assessment and/or a Benefit of the Doubt intervention for your child, you may contact Dr. Falls at:

Phone: 707-525-9300

Email: markfallsphd@gmail.com

Website: fallstherapy.com

Printed in Great Britain
by Amazon